This book is for
Mrs. Chadwick

I hope my book inspires
lots of students to always
look at the positive side of
every situation!

Smile... it will make
you shine!

Maria Elena Cortes
9-28-13

My Annoying Little Brother

In memory of
Maria Ester and Rosario Cortés,
my two loving aunts who inspired me
throughout my childhood.

— M.E.C.

To Leng Chou,
Thanks for caring for me
when I was little and very annoying.
Also, to Bechir, Sami, Tarek,
Aisha, and Malek,
"I love you guys!"

— V.K.

A special thanks to
my two jewels Alexis and Mark,
my cousin Betty,
my sister Monica,
and my mother Teresa
for their patience and support,
and for helping me turn this dream into reality.

Also to
Mary Ann Herrera
Margo & Greg Sedgwick

BOOK DESIGN BY ESTHER SEO

Author photo by Rudy Flores Jr.

Published by Providence Publishing Company
4306 Brook Woods, Houston, TX 77092
(888) 966-3833
Printed in Hong Kong
First Printing 10 9 8 7 6 5 4 3 2

Library of Congress Catalog Card Number 2003111147
My Annoying Little Brother / Marie Elena Cortés / Chris Leathers / Vuthy Kuon
Summary: A young girl complains about her pesky little brother only to realize she cannot live without him.
ISBN 0-9651661-8-x

My Annoying Little Brother

author

Marie Elena Cortés

illustrator

Chris Leathers

produced by

Vuthy Kuon

PROVIDENCE PUBLISHING COMPANY

Houston

I have an annoying little brother!

I HAVE THE BEST BIG SISTER IN THE WORLD!

He follows me around as soon as I get home.

I WANT TO SPEND AS MUCH TIME AS I CAN WITH HER.

He always copies
everything I say.

SHE'S SO GREAT!
I WANT TO BE
JUST LIKE HER.

He draws and scribbles all
over the walls!

HERE'S A PICTURE OF HER. ISN'T SHE BEAUTIFUL?

He loves to make a
big mess in my room!

I LOVE PLAYING
"HIDE & GO SEEK,"
BUT I WONDER WHY
SHE NEVER FINDS ME?

He eats all my chicken nuggets.
SHE SHARES WITH ME
HER FAVORITE FOOD.

But he never touches my salad.

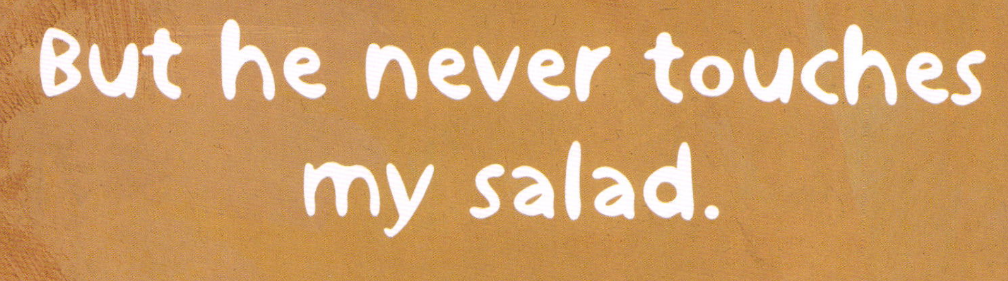

SO I DO THE SAME FOR HER.

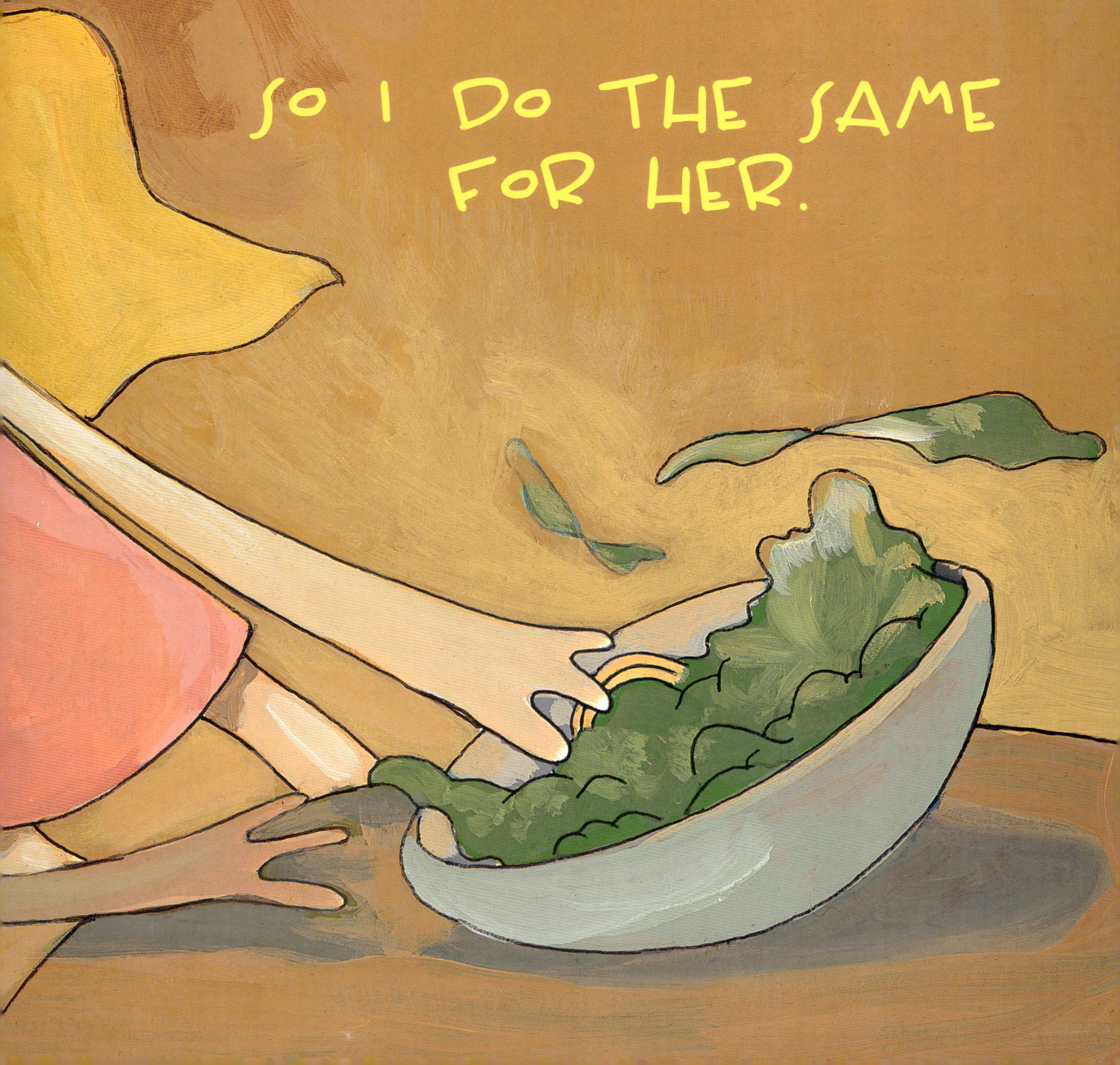

He makes snowmen with my chocolate fudge ice cream.

YUMMY!

He crashes my pajama parties and scares all my friends.

HER FRIENDS LOVE ME. I ALWAYS MAKE THEM LAUGH!

But we always
get him back!

WHY ARE THEY STILL LAUGHING?

He's a pest.
He's a bother.
He's a real pain in the neck!

SHE'S FUN!
SHE'S GREAT!
SHE'S TAUGHT ME
EVERYTHING I KNOW!

And even though he never seems to do anything right...

SHE'S SO SMART,
SHE NEVER DOES
ANYTHING WRONG!

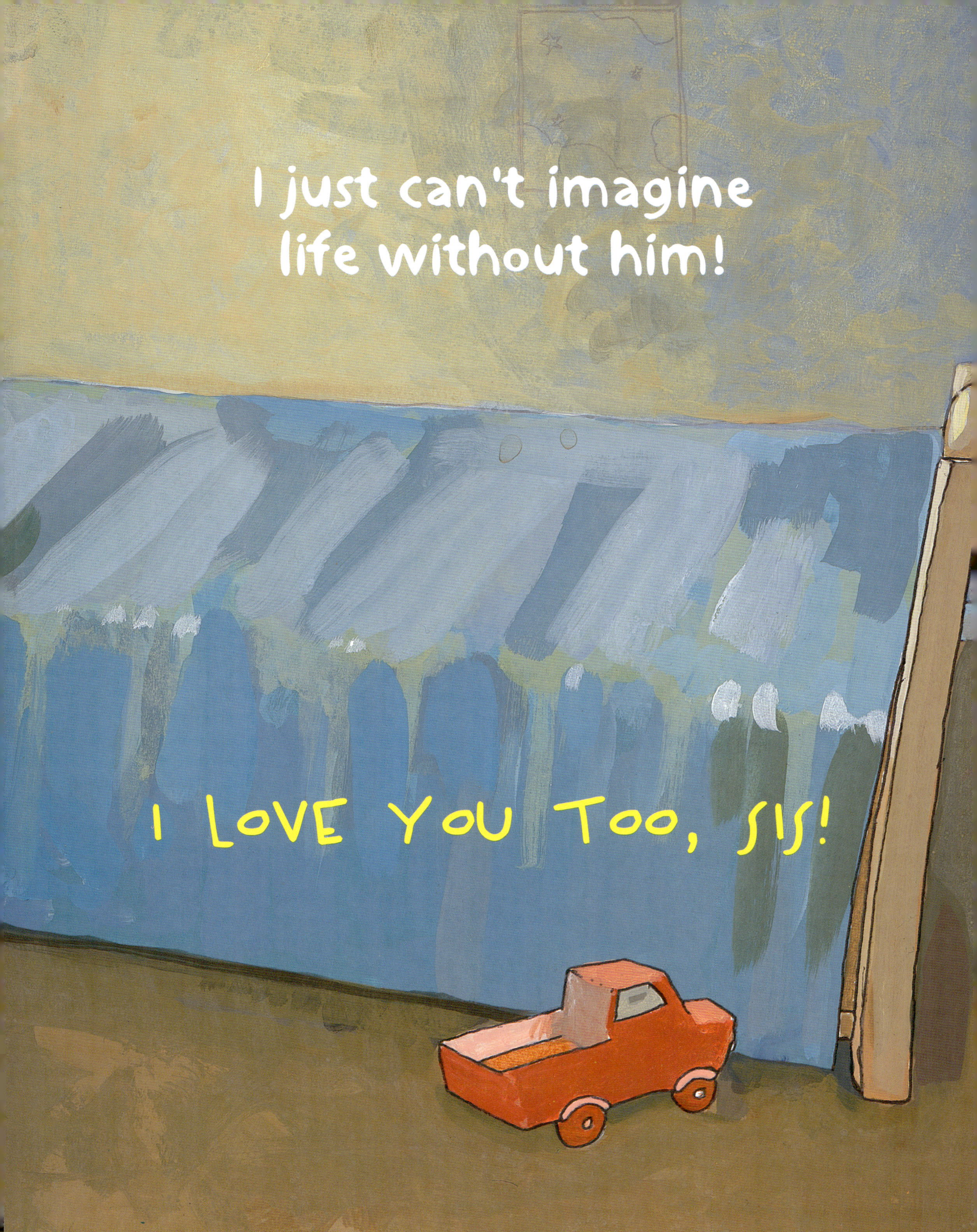
I just can't imagine
life without him!
I LOVE YOU TOO, SIS!

The End